We Were Young

Fortesa Latifi

Edited by Clementine Von Radics

Cover Art by Lindsay Appleby

ISBN: 1519491980
ISBN-13: 9781519491985

"As if this vanishing were progress."

-Mary Karr, *Cherry*

.

I.
the coming apart

ticky

nough, we take the subway

_ ᴜronx and beg a fortuneteller to say the things we need

to hear like one day someone will love us in a way

that we can show our families

and no one will want to cover their mouths.

this time all she says is that I don't have

any color left in my cheeks.

that night, I drink too much and leave blurry

red lip prints on everything I touch

what else is there to do?

I swallowed love whole like a peach,

juice dripping down my face.

the pit is rotting in my stomach

and here I am.

hands still sticky.

heart still reaching

i(phone)

you've left so many angry voicemails

that you're starting to wonder if your

voice ever sounds any other way.

you send a reckless text (read: truthful)

then turn your phone off for three hours.

you change your ringtone so it warns you

when it's actually worth answering.

you're superstitious about what to set as

your background picture so it's never

a person. you don't want to have to change it

later. you use the same emojis

every day and they don't make any

sense. why is the monkey hiding their face?

who are the red lips for?

you change your passcode every time

someone in your family figures it out.

you and your friends get high and talk

about how crazy it is that you have

serious conversations through text messages

and promise to never do it again but still,

that night you all send a series of ones and zeroes

_nrough space and somewhere along the way

they are coded into the perfect words to tell your ex

that you're still angry. you fall asleep

with your phone still in your hand.

2:18 a.m.

you're just kissing the boy so there's really no reas

for him to hold your hand. none of your professors know

your name because you sit in the back of class and only answer

the questions in your head. you can't stop biting your nails

and then panicking about the bacteria on your tongue. at least

twice a day, you think you're about to die. it always comes

as a surprise when you don't. if you're ever bored past 10 o'clock

you fill a mug with watered down vodka and call your exes

but once they answer, you feel sick and rush them off the phone.

you check that the front door is locked no fewer than three times

before bed and still, you can't sleep.

ix

the third rejection letter

the day I get the third rejection letter,

I curl my hair just to feel pretty.

if there's nothing good to feel

at least I can feel pretty.

I have dreams about sleepwalking

where I always tell the truth and end the night

by jumping off the roof of an 18-story building.

you're supposed to wake up before you hit the ground but I don't.

I can't stop crying about how old my grandmother looks

sitting on the subway and whether or not I'll chase love away

by talking about it too much. if at least one spectacular thing

doesn't happen each day, I'm sure nothing good will ever happen

again. I don't know which key goes into which lock

but they're all dangling from my wrist anyway.

yesterday, I taught my niece how to say

I love you and she laughed and laughed.

I wonder who taught me.

x

everyone is terrified

everyone is terrified of your heart reaching through your ribs.

everyone is terrified of the way you love like an open door.

didn't you ever learn you're supposed to guard yourself?

you're supposed to swallow the key or, at the very least, hide it

behind your tongue. when the boys come, you let them kiss you

and you write a poem about it. when the boys come, you think

they're beautiful and forget to look in a mirror for three days.

is that a new freckle or just the imprint of their fingers?

no one can tell but it doesn't matter. you paint your nails a quiet

pink that you hope makes you look less damaged than you are.

you drink a bottle of wine with someone who thinks you're pretty

and dream about the clinking of the glasses for the next week.

brother jimmy's

everyone is pretending to have fun but they can't

stop checking their phones. I want to wipe the hopeful pink

lipstick off the mouth of the girl next to me. I'm one sip away

from telling her she reminds me of a basement with glittering

streamers hanging from the ceiling and a punch bowl in the middle

of the room where the ice is melting and still, no one has shown up

to the party. I tuck a sliver of lemon behind my teeth and consider

kissing the stranger in the corner but can't stand the thought

of him knowing my name so instead I duck into the alley

to throw up, my $7 drink bright blue against the concrete.

girl, this bar wants you to leave. all you have are questions

and all we have are bottles. we don't consider these answers.

you can paint the truth with prom makeup and slip it into

a sparkling dress but it doesn't change anything.

you wouldn't be here so late if you weren't so lonely.

you think we didn't notice?

it's coming off you like perfume.

evidence

I need proof that love can last

so I look everywhere. there is

a package lying neatly on my

doorstep but everything is such

a disappointment these days.

in another world, someone

can't fall asleep without me.

in another world, I swallowed

all my words back, pulling on

them like the string of a balloon.

you didn't deserve it, not any of it,

and I'm sorry to this day.

ıves

I am so reckless-

sweaters, lipstick

so red it's a warning flashing in the night

but no one's paying attention

and it ends up on a boy's shirt collar anyway.

I hurt myself just to prove I can.

I smoke cigarettes I don't want

and drink liquor that comes in plastic bottles.

I fall asleep drunk and screaming at love:

LOOK. YOU'RE NOT THE ONLY ONE

WHO CAN DESTROY ME.

LOOK. I CAN DO IT MYSELF.

mouth wide shut

I won't ever tell them the bad things because I like

being the good one. I like everyone looking at our love

crushed under your feet and knowing it's your fault.

and it is. anything bad I ever did was before I loved you.

there's no excuse for after.

summer air

we're walking to the bar and the soft summer air is

making way for us, parting for our long legs beneath

our light dresses. I'm repeating the birthday on my

fake ID but when we get there, the bartender doesn't

even ask. we sit on the patio and drink frozen margaritas-

mine raspberry, yours blueberry. you stick your tongue

out and the boys at the table next to us laugh. somehow

this starts a conversation where I forget to lie about my

age and they say they won't tell as long as they can buy

us another drink. I laugh because I'm 19 and tipsy

in the city and someone wants to buy me a drink.

my mouth has long since been wiped clean

of my cherry red lipstick and I reapply it in the bathroom,

clumsy and squinting at myself in the mirror.

we leave the bar and walk hand in hand down 33rd

to the dollar pizza place. I ask for extra hot sauce and

don't even care when it drips onto my dress. a night like

any other maybe but in this moment, it feels so special

to hold my best friend's hand and stumble into bed.

when we wake up, my mouth is still red.

history

the last three things I googled: symptoms of anxiety attacks;

how to make eyeliner last longer; the distance between

Los Angeles and Tucson. the saddest thing about growing up

is looking around at my friends and knowing that if I met them

today we wouldn't give a fuck about each other. I'm still young

enough to think that all the bad things people say will happen

won't happen to me like slowly growing apart from the people

you love and spending day after day at a job you don't like.

I'm still young enough to choose cheap wine

and deal with the headache. I'm still young enough

to write poems to find myself and forget to read

between the lines. I wish there were a running tally

of all the affection in my life. I wonder who I've kissed the most.

ephemeral

a child learns to walk for the first time

and stumbles stumbles falls.

we have something in common here

but she has an excuse for it.

I try to remember when to water the plants

and if it's time again to wash the sheets.

people have stopped asking questions.

people have started turning their eyes.

it's too obvious, this hurt, it's too grand

and violent and no one has their sunglasses.

my god, we loved each other, didn't we?

my god, we made a mess of it.

I can see it even now

in the pile of dishes in the sink.

battle

there are seven pill bottles in my purse
and I am embarrassed of all of them.

my body doesn't know how to be a body
without constant reminders.

it's probably my fault.
I taught myself battle so young.

broadway

I.

you get a DUI on Valentine's Day
like some sort of reverse grand gesture-
instead of *look how much I love you*
it's more like *look what a disaster it is*
when I love you.

II.

when you finally hold my hand after five years, I take it
as an insult. I think of crashing my car into your house
and leaving before you come out but instead, I settle
for a quieter cruelty and pull my fingers away.

III.

when I think of how long your mother
has worn her wedding ring
after your father's death
I want to scream.
standing still in time isn't love.
I wish I had learned this earlier.

what depression looks like

carrying a pack of cigarettes and not smoking

them / wearing clothes that are three sizes

too big / losing twenty pounds and laughing

about it / scaring my mother / buying plane tickets

 with the only money I have / crying in the soda aisle

of the grocery store / frantically making plans

and then canceling them / sleeping for five hours

in the middle of the day / draping blankets over

the windows / forgetting the sunscreen / e-mailing

professors about absences / driving towards the mountain

but never up / too much coffee / falling asleep with a cup

of wine next to the bed / the same sweatshirt for weeks

and then suddenly, a new one.

_ngton avenue

in new york, we wear skirts that are too short

and talk to drunk people on the street who want

to know where to find the train. we drink beer

on the roof and talk about what it would take for us

to jump off. we switch boroughs when we're bored

and have a different set of friends in each. we drag

ourselves through the streets until there's no excuse

to be out that late then we laugh in the lobby with

the doorman. we only have to go to the second floor

but we take the elevator anyway and remind ourselves

to stand up straight- after all, there's a camera in the corner.

there was a time

there was a time when we laid on your bed

with the ceiling fan turning in dizzy circles

above our heads and forgot to look at the clock.

there was a time when we drank the kind of wine

that gives you a sweet ache in your teeth

and talked about the people we loved before

we knew each other existed. there was a time

when we felt so safe in your cheap apartment

with the front door locked against the past.

if someone would have told me that in two

years time, I would be doing the same thing

across town in a different bed,

this time whispering your name

when I counted old hurts,

I would have screamed.

II.
the reckoning

the truth

you fell apart in my hands

like fruit I waited too long to eat

reflections on femininity

I.

I feel most feminine when there is blood.

I put on mascara three different times before

I leave the house and still check it in the rearview.

I get by on being pretty. it makes people stick around

until they find something else

to like about me.

II.

 I can be so cruel when you love me.

I'll laugh when you say it and ignore you for a week.

when we talk again, I'll drink too much and hold your hand

then fall asleep in your bed and leave before you wake up

then text you something stupid like

how's your hangover?

III.

I want to be one of those girls who grow three inches

when it's time to stand up for myself. I don't want to

excuse your behavior with the fact that I love you.

at some point, that should stop mattering.

wreckage

we want to be ruined.

there is something that

appeals to us about being

the main character in a story

this awful. we put on our best

dresses and wait in the street.

you'll destroy us and afterward

we'll kiss your neck.

college

growing up means choosing sleep over your friends
and buying close-toed shoes in bland colors. I miss
how wild we used to be, tapping a keg on a Wednesday
and letting our shower drain clog for months at a time.
we had a 4-bedroom apartment and still fell asleep
together in your bed. once, we went to philosophy 101 drunk
and thought we had it all figured out. once, we invited four boys
to the same party and ignored all of them. once, we woke up to
graffiti on my car and screamed. now, my alarm is set for 6:30
and I eat sliced fruit for breakfast. we see each other once a week
when we have time but usually we don't have time.
I can't remember the last time we stayed awake
until morning. I can't remember the last time
I laughed without worrying what I looked like.

secondhand

when I was 10, my brother accidentally told me

my grandfather had died in front of the neighbors

and I cried into my cereal. tragedy has always

come to me like that- secondhand, a story that has

already rested in so many other ears. I can't be trusted

to handle it because I'll probably do something awful

like shatter all the plates I own and walk across the shards

then write a poem about how the glass feels

sticking to the bottom of my feet.

not everything has to be romantic.

sometimes death is just death.

the city

I love the city like a bruise I can't keep
my hands off of.

once, at a bar uptown,
I lost my leather jacket and the moment
I decided I'd be okay without it
I found it again.

once, I fell asleep on the F train
and woke up in the neighborhood
where I first learned how to walk.

once, I slipped in the snow
and grabbed the first hand I saw.

the city waits for me like nothing else ever has.
every time I return, there is a different group of people
idling outside the airport. sometimes they don't even last the visit
and when it comes time to leave,
I kiss only the buildings goodbye.

twenty-two

we want to be brave so we lie to ourselves

because most of the time that's what being

brave is. we worry about the same things

we've always worried about, only now

it's all the time. we feel ourselves getting older

in small ways like caring about organic

groceries and falling asleep after two drinks

and it scares us so we drink a whole pitcher

of too sweet margaritas and smoke

on the porch just like old times

but in our minds we're already calculating

how many hours of sleep we can get

before work in the morning. the next day,

we watch high school kids sitting next to us

in traffic. they roll down the windows, light

their cheap cigarettes and turn up their music.

we cringe.

resistance

in this apartment, there are boys who take offense to anyone

calling them boys. they grow out their beards and never do the

dishes. they've taken up smoking but only recently.

look at the way they hold the cigarette between their fingers-

they aren't used to it yet but they will be. there's a bong

in the living room and joints in their pockets. at the end

of the week, they have a party and drink until one of them

falls over the balcony. the back brace keeps his spine straight

for three months but the moment it's taken off

he slumps over again.

body part II

I am always begging my body not to be so broken

but my body just laughs because it knows who started

this war. on days like this, I am ashamed to look in the

mirror so I lie in bed and pretend to be someone else.

the pretending is another thing to be ashamed of but

that is a story for another day. everything I've ever

wanted is still miles away from my outstretched hands

and I'm beginning to question the point of desire

which probably means things are getting bad again

but sometimes there are more practical things to consider

like co-pays and insurance companies so I stay in bed.

if only things would hurt in a clearer way, I might be able

to talk about it instead of crying anytime I get the chance.

every tear means the same thing: *you are weak. small.*

you will never find your way out of this.

sepia

looking back, everything is sepia to me now-

the pills, the shaking, the undressing, your neck

in the shadow of the lost night, the pills, your hair

cut over the bathroom sink, the broken front door,

the cigarettes sleeping in the makeshift ashtray, the pills,

your crooked front tooth, the sunset smeared on the windows

the miles ticking by until the odometer sputtered and choked,

tired of counting how far I would run to catch you, the pills,

the pills, the pills, how young we were, how wild, how tired,

how loud in our aching, how insistent the world stop to listen to

our hearts smashing against the ground like glittering pieces of the

last mirror we recognized ourselves in.

all that was once so bright-

it's sepia to me now.

coping

there is a kind of sleep I only fall into

when bad things have happened.

I am not graceful with pain.

once, during the worst time,

my sister came to my apartment

and said I know you're having

a shitty time but you still need

to brush your hair. instead,

I let it knot. instead, my mother

drips honey into warm milk

and holds my head in her lap.

instead, I cry thick mascara tears

and blame it on the weather.

there is somewhere I am trying

to get back to but I can only see

it in my dreams. when I wake up

my hands are shaking again.

86th street

my grandmother has lived in Brooklyn longer than she

has lived anywhere else but still refuses to twist her tongue

around English words too often. I admire her for this.

I have written two books she can't read. she curses

more than my brother does because it makes us all laugh.

my grandmother can tell you how to put a baby to sleep

and how to make yogurt using only milk and the stovetop

and also how to love your children even when you don't like them.

once, she came to visit and gave me a gold bracelet and slept

in my bed for a month. once, I drove four hours through a storm

to find her alone in a 5-bedroom house. once, I came home at 6 in

the morning and found her slicing fruit at the kitchen table and

crying into the cracks I kissed her forehead and she told me I

smelled like cigarettes. two showers later, I still couldn't

get the smell out of my hair.

we promised

I am not always proud of the people I love.

sometimes I want to grab them by the shoulders

and shake them until they remember everything

they wanted to be when they were young

and untouched. I want to say remember

when you were 10 and you swore you'd never

smoke cigarettes? now there is always a lighter

in your pocket. remember when you thought the boys

you loved would always bring flowers on your birthday

and open the car door for you to step in? we were

floating in my pool, small bodies pale against the

bright blue of the water and you laughed and said

that you'd marry someone who never yelled and always

remembered your favorite flavor of ice cream.

remember when we were teenagers shot gunning beers

in a house we'd never been to before and you said it was

all just for fun? remember how we used to fantasize

about being old enough to have our own cars? we promised

we would wash them every week and they would always smell like

evergreen or maybe peppermint but it's been months now.

we can barely see through the dust.

fingertips

you never thought your body could be

anything except bruised. your locked door.

your haunted house. the unlearning

is taking so long.

girl

the first time I ever wore a bra, I fidgeted the whole day.

I sat at the art table in 5th grade and tried to figure out

the best way to adjust it without the boys noticing.

12 years later and the underwire is still cutting into my skin.

the first time I ever carried a purse, it felt like an extra limb.

didn't know what to put in it but I knew it should be full.

open that first bag and you would find a pack of gum,

a tube of half-melted chapstick and a watermelon-shaped coin

purse.

the first time I ever wore makeup, I forgot my new face

and rubbed my hands over my eyes.

when I got home, I washed my skin

with a hot cloth until it was bright red and mine again.

home

home is at least 3,000 miles away at any given moment.

it is not easy to know where to be once people stop

telling you. we asked for this and now that it's here,

we don't know what to do with it. we find ourselves

looking through old photo albums and envying our

younger selves which is not a comfortable feeling.

once, in a lecture, a professor named the exact

sensation. exaltation of the past: the tendency to

view the past as ideal and feel the intense desire

to return to it. even last month seems perfect

and today, hopeless already.

the truth in two parts

the good news is I survived knowing you.

the bad news is you were something

I had to survive

II.
the glistening

albatross

since your first taste, you never wanted

to do without it. you're clumsy in love

falling into it like the summer you stumbled

into a cactus during a game of tag

and had to pull the stickers out one by one.

you, with your albatross heart.

you could live on love.

facebook thinks you know this person

you should be angrier, but you're not. in this situation,

people expect you to scream or throw something but

mostly you're just crying at stoplights with the windows

rolled up. you are supposed to feel something sharp,

something you can use as a tool, but you just ache

which is no use at all. years after the fact, you still

find yourself feeling sick when you realize all that is left

of you and the person you loved are rotting apologies

thrown across state lines. there was a better way for this

to end but you can't change the story or explain it away.

mostly, it comes down to this: there are things that grow

with water and there are things that drown. in this story,

he is the water and depending on the day, you can either

breathe or you can't.

body

better people have died for lesser things and here I am,

throwing myself off of cliffs, eating only grapes and lettuce

for eight seasons in a row, cringing when my heel bones sigh

and crack underneath me, laughing at my ribs sticking through

my skin, driving too fast, comparing my heart to the steering

wheel of the first car I ever wrecked.

my parents turn to each other at night and wonder

what this says about me. it isn't good, they know.

there is supposed to be an evolutionary desire to survive

and of their five children, it seemed this skipped only me.

girl, disturbed

our tights are ripping at our thighs

and settling into the cuts in our hips

but we won't notice the blood until later.

we'll skip the winter coat and take

a sore throat instead. when it snows

on st. patrick's day, we take it

as an excuse to drink. we sit on the bar

and wrap our legs around the stools.

there are people here who want

to kiss us but we know better.

they would settle for holding our hands

but we flinch.

the moment we know each other most

when the girl you love dies and there is

only rain to keep her company.

when there's a crash and you kill

a man at a bus stop and wake up in handcuffs.

when your parents look into your eyes

and find your brother's ghost.

when your parents don't look into your eyes

at all. when your father commits the slowest

suicide possible and you have to watch

because no one else will and death should

have an audience. when you divorce for the

second time and everyone sighs. when someone

you love doesn't love you. when your body falls

apart slice by slice and you don't know where your

knees are. I meant to call to tell you that we found

your elbow in the bottom of the swimming pool

but I wasn't sure if you would want it back.

we're the adults

we're the adults here so we take naps in the

middle of the afternoon with the window open.

there's an ice cream truck singing down the street

and I haven't hung up my clothes. I text your mother

a picture of you on your first day of work and say

isn't he handsome. our toothbrushes sitting in a cup

on the edge of the sink are the most intimate thing

I have ever known.

tucson, arizona

this city, the belly of the desert

a mirage in a painted pool.

this city, lying on its stomach

as the heat stretches over the pavement.

a tarantula surrenders under a car tire

a child burns her hands on the monkey bars

teenagers kiss in the cacti

the sun sets like a melted popsicle

dripping down tired hands.

in the street, a boy learns how to drive,

turns the wrong way and falls into a lake

with no water. the girl who loves him can't find

him so she climbs to the top of the mountain

and throws herself off. she lands right next to him.

a toad sings them to sleep. coyotes tiptoe around

their bodies. the neighbors sigh and say the heat,

the heat, it does strange things to people.

maybe the people were already strange.

maybe the people always wanted something

to dive off a mountain for.

friendship bracelets

mostly, we pitch tents in the desert

when we want to feel alive and try

a new drug and laugh at how it makes us

feel and hold hands walking across the street

and trade makeup and start the car just to charge

our phones and squint through the soap falling into

our eyes. mostly, we get drunk on cheap wine and say

remember that boy we thought we loved but then

he ended up being awful and remember that boy who loved

us but then we ended up being awful and remember

when we were just kids but we thought we weren't

and the keys to our first cars felt like passports and school

was just a thing we had to get through before our lives began?

mostly, we listen to music and smoke on balconies and meet

strangers at parties and drive home so late that the businessman

in the car next to us is already having his first cup of coffee.

mostly, we're just trying to feel okay.

most days, this is enough.

I.

swamp cooler humming

in the corner. a glass of wine

sweating on the table.

this is the second summer

we've been in love.

II.

when the world is this feverish

I think of water blisters,

towels laid flat on leather seats,

and the first morning we woke up

together.

III.

I leave letters around your room

and on every page, only this:

everything is better now.

euclid

at a party, I repeat the same three facts

about myself and other people pretend

I'm interesting. when it's my turn to pretend,

I refill my drink. in the kitchen, a ping pong ball

bounces against the dirty tiles and no one thinks

twice about drinking the beer it sinks into.

in the backyard two people who just met kiss

for the first and only time. on the front porch

two girls fight over who is sober enough to drive.

in the living room a boy teaches a girl a drinking game

she has never played before and she tries to pay attention.

in the bathroom, two kids hunch over a small lump of coke

balanced on a key. I refill my drink until I can't remember

the three facts anymore. when someone asks, I just wait

for the moment to pass.

o turn right to go to the airport

urned it off? what if we kept driving and

ur hand was always on my leg and we never got

the sand out of our hair? I know that I should be

mature and kiss you without my hands on your face

and walk to the terminal with a straight back but I can't

stop thinking about your ocean glass eyes.

I love you and sometimes I'm sloppy about it

but I think that's okay because no one ever wrote about

a love that didn't get a little messy sometimes.

let's not turn right. left feels better.

left leaves me with you.

family

in my family

we catch airplanes

to be there for the

important moments.

in my family

we have brown eyes

and blue and green

and we all look the same

or in some light, completely

different.

in my family

we wear each other's clothes

and sleep in each other's beds

and grind the coffee beans

the night before so we don't

wake each other up.

in my family

we put our feet on the table

and eat in the backyard

and grow tomatoes in the garden.

when we're all together

I can't believe that this all started

because my parents fell in love

as college students.

when I think of it this way

I feel something close to hope.

reckless

we are reckless with each other

because we are young and we don't know yet

how damage can last, how it can grow and spread

and unfurl through a life like the roots of a tree

finding its way through the dirt. for now, it's a way

to amuse ourselves, playing games using each other

as discolored stand-ins for who we really wish was

holding our hand. this will do for now because

we are young and we haven't found a way to be brave

about being alone so we use each other in awful ways

and laugh when we wake up and give it a rest until

the weekend rolls around again and our beds feel

so desperately empty that we have to fill them.

this will do for now, but not much longer.

passing

the easy part is over

and we can't stop looking back

to figure out exactly

when it happened.

in separate apartments

scattered around the same city

we mourn.

there was a time when this

would have been unimaginable.

we get together and pretend

it's the same but even a stranger

looking in could see it's hollow.

some days I feel like the stranger.

some days I can't even look.

panic attack

in the middle of the night, you lie in a bed t

but feels just as good and you hyperventila

but spreads quickly, like a fever in the sum....

later, when it gets bad enough, you wake the person you love

and he turns to you and says your name over and over

and you wonder how he knew that you weren't sure you existed

at all. he tells you to repeat after him and you do. your voices

slow dance together in the darkness and quietly, your breath comes

back. he waits for you to throw up in the bathroom and he lets you

leave the light on. he is so tired that his body is angry at him

for letting it be kept awake but he is patient. only when you are

next to him under the covers and breathing a soft flow

of in and out does he sleep again. when you wake in the morning,

it feels as though nothing has happened at all.

rt

pull the table into the corner of the room

and lay the comforter down on the wood floor.

I get the pillows and you open the wine.

I wrap my body around yours and sigh into

your chest. when you laugh catches in your throat

I want to trap it in a jar and listen to it later.

no one every says what a miracle it is to be in love

and not suffer for it but every time I look at you,

I know. I would fall asleep on the floor every night

if it meant resting my head in our love.

tubac

he rolls a joint with his thick boy fingers

and buys a baguette at the corner store.

he crosses county lines and we're waiting.

we make dinner and are stupidly proud

when it requires more than three ingredients.

afterwards, the drinking game goes on for two hours

until everything is blurry. this is what we wanted.

the next morning we jump into the pool one after another

and call ourselves cleansed.

To my parents Rifat & Drita Latifi for the endless love, support, and laughter and for creating the beautiful family that is the center of everything I am. To my siblings Tina, Qesa, Kush, & Luli- I couldn't do anything without knowing you're by my side. I love you always. Linda, for holding my hand no matter where I lead us and being my best friend since the day I was born. Alex, for being my safe place. Neeaz, for being the first person I gave handwritten poems to back in elementary school. Blake, for being my creative other half and for reading the many different versions of these poems with incredible patience. Trista, for always answering the phone.

& you, always, for reading.

about the author

Fortesa Latifi is a 22-year old poet who calls the desert home. She is a graduate of the University of Arizona. This is her second book. Her work has been featured in Persona, Words Dance, Femrat, Kosovo 2.0, Rising Phoenix, Vagabond City Lit, The Fem Lit Mag, and To Write Love On Her Arms. She hopes this book reminds you of being young and having lipstick smudged on your teeth. She hopes you find what you need here. For more of her work, you can visit madgirlf.tumblr.com

Made in the USA
Middletown, DE
17 November 2016